DESTINY COMES WITH PAIN

The Price of Purpose and Greatness

OMOLABAKE OLAOYE
COACH OMO

ACKNOWLEDGMENTS

To those who stayed when I was silent and believed when I couldn't speak for myself, this is for you.

Writing this book was more than simply putting words on paper. It was pouring out pieces of my soul. I wrote some chapters through tears. Some go through prayer. Some battles I fought silently, never shared publicly. But each one carried a weight I could not bear alone.

To God, my anchor and my author—thank You for trusting me with this message. Thank you for turning every scar into a sentence and every tear into a teaching. Now I understand that none of it went to waste. Though you broke me, you rebuilt me stronger. You hid me only to release me at the right time. You've been faithful in every season.

To my family, thank you for loving me through all my developing versions. For your patience, your prayers, and your presence. You've been my safe place in the chaos. I'm forever grateful.

To my mentors, coaches, and spiritual leaders—thank you for holding me accountable, for pushing me when I wanted to settle, and for reminding me who I am when life tried to convince me otherwise.

To my team at Eclat and Evolvance, thank you for embodying the vision of excellence. Your faith in this message made it possible to bring this book to life. Your support behind the scenes has been my quiet strength.

To my readers and clients, past and present—your stories, your faith, your fight to keep becoming even when it hurts... inspired every word in this book. You are proof that pain has a purpose.

To those who walked away, thank you. Your absence taught me to discern wisely. Your silence revealed the power of God's voice. And your departure made space for the right people to walk in.

Finally, to you, dear reader—thank you for welcoming my words into your sacred space. Thank you for trusting me with your story as I shared parts of mine. I do not take it lightly.

If this book reflected your pain, I pray it also opened a window to your purpose.

From my heart to yours,
Coach Omo.

FOREWORD

By Jimi Tewe

There comes a time in every person's journey when reflection becomes essential. Deep, soul-level evaluation, not just casual thinking, awakens the existence and challenges of who you have become.

That is precisely what this book achieves.

From the very first page, it offers a firm yet gentle invitation to pause, breathe, and take an honest look at your life. In a world that constantly celebrates hustle and praises perfection, this message boldly reminds people that their worth does not depend on how much they do, but on how fully they live—aligned, aware, and free.

This book is not a motivational speech wrapped in pages. It is not a superficial pep talk designed to make you feel good temporarily. What you hold here is a guide for realignment. It is a healing tool. It is a declaration that you may rediscover yourself—without shame or guilt, and without the pressure to perform.

The words here will not only speak to your mind but will also touch your spirit. Each chapter has vulnerability, wisdom, and grace. There is clarity. There is a process. And most importantly, there is hope.

To the women who will encounter this book, I urge you to read it slowly. Let it interrupt your cycles. Let it challenge every false narrative you have believed about yourself. And then, let it guide you back home to yourself.

This is more than a book. It is a journey. It is a restoration of hope. And I believe with all my heart that if you embrace what is within these pages, you will not remain the same.

Enjoy every page.
Jimi Tewe
Global Speaker. Transformation Strategist, Nation Builder.

FOREWORD

By Peter Fashola

People often say the road to greatness is difficult. But what if your current pain isn't a setback, but a setup? Could it be the very thing that's breaking you, shaping you into the person you've become?

In the pages that follow, you will come face-to-face with a truth that many of us wish was not so—that destiny comes with pain. Difficulty, struggle, and challenges truly refine us. Amid rejection, betrayal, loss, and heartache, God is not absent. No, He is at work, preparing you for the greatness that He has destined you for.

As you read this book, you will discover something that will change your perspective forever: Pain is not your enemy. It is a partner in your growth. Pain is the furnace that tests your character, solidifies your faith, and births your purpose. It's not about avoiding pain; it's about learning to navigate it with faith and resilience.

This journey is not for the faint of heart. Reflecting on the stories shared in this book, I remember those who came before us—Joseph, whom his brothers betrayed; all these individuals experienced pain, but it was in pain that they discovered the fullness of their purpose.

As you progress through this book's chapters, keep in mind: Your pain signals progress, not failure. It shows you're on a path of growth for a purpose greater than you realise. Don't let the burdens of the journey overshadow the greatness awaiting you. You weren't meant to break; you were meant to evolve.

This book is for the dreamers and fighters who are ready to face storms to find the rainbow. Whether you're dealing with betrayal, waiting, or loneliness, remember that God is with you and is preparing you for something greater than what you see now.

So, I challenge you to read this book with an open heart and a steadfast spirit. Let it remind you that pain is a tool, not a weapon against you. It's the very thing that will position you for greatness.

Some books inform, and some books transform. This one does both—gracefully, honestly, and powerfully. As I turned the pages of this remarkable work, I sensed the heartbeat of a nation, the cry of a generation, and the whisper of healing rising from the cracks of broken words.

We are living in a time where people weaponise words, vandalise identities, and paralyse destinies because we've underestimated the healing power of words. But this book? It stands as a defiant lighthouse in a stormy sea, calling the drifting soul back to purpose, restoration, and dignity.

Destiny comes with pain. But let me tell you, the price of purpose is worth every tear, every setback, and every sacrifice. The world is waiting for you to step into your destiny. Are you ready?

So, read these pages slowly. Read them prayerfully. Read them aloud if you must. Let each phrase wash over your soul like morning rain on parched land. And then, speak those words into your relationships, your communities, your nations.

Because when words heal, nations rise.

This is more than a book; it is a movement.

A restoration movement.

A revolution in voice.

A revival of hope.

Welcome to the healing.
Chap. (CPT) Peter Fasola
US Army Chaplain Corps.

FOREWORD

By David Shiyanbade

Pain is one of life's most relentless teachers. It is not God's preferred method to teach, train, transform, or grow His children. However, like anything else, when yielded to the Holy Spirit, it can turn out for our good (Romans 8:28 NLT). It arrives uninvited, sometimes lingers longer than we wish because of our response and handling of it, and often leaves us questioning its purpose. Yet, through the lens of Scripture, we learn that pain is not punishment but consequence, and it produces refinement.

> *"He will sit as a refiner and purifier of silver..."*
> (Malachi 3:3 NLT).

This verse reveals a sacred truth: God does not stand afar off when we face challenging circumstances. Like a master refiner, He patiently observes and tends near us, ensuring we lose nothing in the fire. The flames do not consume us; they shape us. The heat does not destroy us; it reveals His image within us.

This book is an invitation to walk through that refining fire—not merely the fire of affliction but the fire of transformation (Psalm 34:19-20 NLT). It explores how God's trials strip away our diminishment and awaken our innate brilliance. Like the Levites of old, we too are being purified so that our lives might rise as offerings holy, acceptable, and radiant before Him.

As you turn these pages, may you see that the heat you feel is not evidence of abandonment but of God's attentive hand at work. The process of refinement is happening within you. You are being made whole. You are being prepared for the next season (John 16:33 NLT).

In a world that teaches us to hide our wounds, avoid discomfort, and glorify only the mountaintop moments, we must not forget: pain, when handled with courage and faith, can become the soil where strength, wisdom, and new life take root.

This book does not deny the reality of suffering, nor

does it glorify hardship. Instead, it offers a vision of transformation; how loss, disappointment, heartbreak, and struggles can become catalysts for resilience, compassion, and deeper purpose. Each chapter invites you to see adversity not as a wall but as a doorway. On the other side lies growth, healing, and a truer version of yourself.

The path will not always be straightforward. Refinement never is. But it is worth it. For in God's hands, even pain redeems for glory. If you are holding this book, chances are you are seeking more than relief; you are seeking meaning, hope, and a way forward. Within these pages, you will find all of that and more.

May this work remind you of this unshakable truth: pain is not the end of your story. It is often at the very beginning. The pain is never the ultimate word; God is.

David Shiyanbade
Pastor, Teacher and Coach Congress of Saviours International.

FOREWORD

By Oyinlola Bukky Akande

'*Destiny Comes with Pain*' is a powerful book about the actual cost of becoming who you are. It shows that pain is often a part of the journey to greatness. If you have ever wondered why your path feels more challenging than others or why you have faced so many struggles, this book will help you understand why.

Through real-life stories, Bible examples, and honest reflections, the book explains how rejection, delay, heartbreak, and loneliness can all shape you for a greater purpose. It teaches that pain is not a punishment but a process that prepares you for the future.

This book is not about avoiding suffering. It is about learning to grow through it. It will help you see that the challenges you face are not a sign that you are off track. They may be the very things that are guiding you into your true calling. If you feel stuck, lost, or tired of waiting, this book is for you. It will help you find meaning in your pain, give you hope, and remind you that you are not alone. Most of all, it will encourage you to keep going, because your destiny is worth it.

Oyinlola Bukky Akande
Serial networker, Life-Coach, Speaker, Author, Publisher, Consultant, Opportunity Broker, Bridge Builder and Event Enthusiast.

INTRODUCTION

The Hidden Cost of Destiny

Have you ever felt like your journey is more complicated than others'? Have you faced rejection, betrayal, delays, and struggles that made you question whether you are on the right path? If so, take comfort in knowing that you are not alone. Destiny involves pain, and it's a shared experience among those who are on the path to greatness.

From the moment you were born, your life has had a purpose. Chance did not create you, and your existence isn't random. However, what many people cannot realise is that a great destiny does not come easily. Trials, pain, and perseverance build it. The greater the calling, the greater the obstacles you will encounter.

Society often presents us with the illusion that success comes easily, that all we need to do is work hard, be good, and everything will fall into place. But the truth is quite different. Every great person, every impactful leader, and everyone who has truly followed their purpose has faced seasons of deep pain.

'Pain is not a sign that you are on the wrong path; it is often the confirmation that you are walking toward your purpose.'

Let's read Daniel's story:

Daniel's Story

As a child, Daniel always felt different. While his friends dreamt of becoming doctors, engineers, or celebrities, he wasn't sure what he wanted to be. But deep inside, there was always this sensation, a strange, unshakeable pull towards something greater. He didn't know what it was, but he felt it.

Life, however, did not unfold as he had expected. Hardship filled his teenage years. His father abandoned the family, leaving his mother to raise him and his siblings alone. They had barely enough to eat, and he often went to bed hungry. He watched his mother cry when she thought no one was looking. The pain of those years made him angry. He wondered why life had to be so difficult.

By the time he turned 18, Daniel had one goal: to escape his suffering. He threw himself into making money, pursuing any opportunity that promised success. He started a business, and then another. Some failed, some thrived, but no matter how much he earned, something inside him felt empty.

In his late twenties, he met an old mentor at a small café. After catching up, the mentor asked a question that changed everything, reminding him he was born for something bigger.

"Daniel, what are you chasing?"

Daniel laughs bitterly. "Success, money, a good life. Isn't that what we all want?"

His mentor shook his head. *There is a difference between ambition and destiny. Ambition is about what you want. Destiny describes the purpose of your creation. You've been running all these years, but have you ever stopped to ask, what is my purpose?*

Daniel remained silent. He had never considered it from that perspective.

The mentor continued, *"True destiny doesn't come easy. It comes with pain, struggle, and sacrifice. That is why so many people avoid it. But the ones who embrace it... they change the world."*

That night, Daniel couldn't sleep. He reflected on his life, the suffering, the hunger, the failures. What if none of it was meaningless? What if the pain was guiding him towards something greater?

He realised something profound: his struggles were shaping him for a purpose he had been avoiding.

The Unseen Side of Destiny

Many individuals, such as Daniel, avoid their true destiny because it entails suffering and hardship. They find it simpler to chase after ambition, wealth, success, and comfort rather than confront the difficulties associated with fulfilling their purpose.

But here's the truth: **if you are called to something great, you will go through great pain.**

Reflect on this: everyone who pursues his or her destiny encounters hardships before achieving success.

- **Nelson Mandela spent 27 years in prison before leading South Africa to freedom.**
- **Oprah Winfrey faced childhood trauma and career rejection before rising to become a global icon.**
- **Before Joseph (Biblical figure) became a ruler, his brothers betrayed him, sold him into slavery, and imprisoned him.**

- **Before fulfilling His most extraordinary mission, people rejected, beat, and crucified Jesus Christ.**

Is there anyone else in your life at the moment that you can think of? None of them had a straightforward path. Why? Destiny must shape you first before it reveals you. This means that the challenges and pain you experience are not random or pointless; they have a purpose. They are part of a process that is moulding you into the person you need to be to fulfil your destiny.

Why Your Pain Is Necessary for Destiny

Pain is not **punishment**; it is **preparation**. It's the fire that refines you, shaping you into a stronger, wiser, and more resilient version of yourself. If you received your destiny without going through the fire, you wouldn't be strong enough to handle it. Just as fire purifies gold, your pain prepares you to reach your full potential.

Consider this:

Shaped by pain, you gain resilience, wisdom, and emotional strength.

Pain separates you – it removes people and distractions that are not meant for your journey.
Pain redirects you – it guides you away from what is temporary and towards what is eternal.

Without pain, you would not develop the strength, wisdom, and endurance needed to handle your destiny.

Pain also **separates you from the ordinary**. Not everyone will endure hardship, and many people give up when it becomes tough. But those who persevere through the pain, who refuse to be defeated, rise above the rest. They are the ones genuinely prepared to bear the weight of their calling.

Many believe that struggle shows they are going the wrong way. However, often, struggle shows you are on the right track.

Pain serves a purpose; it refines, strengthens, and prepares you for the weight of your calling. If you are experiencing deep struggles right now, I want you to consider this:

- **Rejection is merely redirection. You were never destined to keep the person who walked away from you in your future.**
- **Delay is part of preparation. The thing you've been awaiting is being refined so that when it arrives, you'll be ready to manage it.**
- **Loneliness is growth. Sometimes, God removes people from your life so you can focus on becoming the person you are.**
- **Pain is part of the process. Every challenge, heartbreak, and setback shapes you for something greater.**

Embracing the Journey Ahead

This book goes beyond recognising pain; it focuses on understanding and embracing it. It encourages viewing suffering not as punishment but as an essential part of reaching greatness. The goal is to shift your perspective and handle pain confidently without losing faith in your purpose.

In the upcoming chapters, we will examine the various pains associated with destiny, from rejection and loneliness to waiting and sacrifice. More importantly, we will explore ways to overcome these hardships so that you can fully embrace the extent of your calling.

Perhaps you've asked yourself, "Why am I going through this?" This book is for you. If you have ever felt like giving up, this book is for you. If you know deep down that more was meant for you, but the journey feels unbearable, this book is for you.

Let's undertake this journey together. Your destiny is worth the effort.

A Challenge for You

As you start this book, take a moment to reflect on your journey. Write the biggest struggles you've faced and ask yourself:

1. What lessons has this pain taught me?
2. How has my suffering shaped me into a stronger person?
3. Am I willing to endure temporary pain for the sake of my long-term destiny?

Your **mindset shift begins now. Let's dive in.**

PART ONE

The Nature of Destiny and Pain

2

Chapter 1

WHAT IS DESTINY?

Understanding Your Life's Purpose

Have you ever asked yourself, 'Why am I here? What is my purpose? Am I meant for something greater?' These are questions everyone considers in life. Destiny encompasses more than just success, wealth, or fame;

Often, people overlook the truth that nobody guarantees destiny. Being destined for greatness doesn't mean success will come; it requires effort, struggle, and sacrifice. Many have the potential but cannot realise their destiny because they are unwilling to face the obstacles that lie ahead.

This chapter will explore the true meaning of destiny, how to identify it, and why it often involves hardship and effort.

Defining Destiny: More Than Just a Dream

Destiny is the realisation of your purpose. It explains the creator's reason for your creation and the unique path for you to follow. It is not merely about reaching goals but about fulfilling the greater contribution your life makes to the world.

Your destiny is:

- **Preordained**: You were created with a specific mission in mind.
- **Unique**: No one else has your exact path, skills, or purpose.
- **Bigger Than You**: Your destiny is not just about personal success, but about.

For example, a doctor's destiny is not just to earn money but to heal people. A teacher's destiny is not just to get a paycheck but to shape minds. Your destiny always has a greater purpose than just benefitting yourself. Many people confuse destiny with ambition. Ambition is what you desire; destiny is what you achieve. While ambition arises from personal wishes, destiny is often something more profound—something you feel called to do, even when it is difficult.

Destiny Vs Ambition

Many people confuse destiny with ambition, believing them to be the same. Although both involve a desire for success and achievement, their origins, purposes, and effects are different. Recognising the difference between the two is essential for understanding whether you are pursuing personal goals or discovering your true calling. Let's examine the difference between destiny and ambition.

What Is Destiny?

- Destiny is the **divinely ordained path for your life**, the purpose you fulfil.
- It preordains and is deeply connected to your unique gifts, calling, and contribution to the world.
- Destiny is **greater than personal success**; it is about **impact, service, and legacy.**
- It is not always what you want, but what destiny intends for you
-

Nelson Mandela's destiny was not just to be a lawyer. His destiny was to fight for justice and free his people.

What Is Ambition?

- Ambition is an **intense desire for personal success, achievement, or status.**
- It is **self-driven**, based on personal desires, dreams, and aspirations.
- External elements (money, power, fame frequently judged ambition, recognition).

- While ambition can be noble, people often focus on personal advancement rather than making a meaningful impact with it.

A person may be ambitious to become a millionaire, but if wealth is his or her only goal, it is not necessarily his or her destiny; it is just a personal pursuit.

The Source
— Divine Calling vs. Personal Desire

"Many are the plans in a person's heart, but it is the Lord's purpose that prevails."
Proverbs 19:21

We all have dreams. From a young age, we're taught to aim high, work hard, and achieve success. And there's nothing wrong with dreaming or wishing for a better life. But there is a difference between what we desire and **what we are truly called to do.**

In a society focussed on self-promotion, immediate gratification, and curated social media lives, it's common to confuse personal wishes with a divine vocation. However, the true origin of your journey influences its strength, durability, and significance. **A holy calling guides you toward purpose, while personal desire pushes you toward success.**

Let me show you the difference—not only in theory, but through the story of two lives.

Ambition's Chase: The Story of Lara

Lara was a talented speaker. From her teenage years, she could command a room with her words. Her voice possessed natural authority, and her storytelling drew people in. However, somewhere along the way, Lara dreamt not of transforming lives but of gaining recognition. She idolised influencers and coaches with millions of followers, flashy cars, and fully booked events.

Her dream changed from **having a purpose to seeking popularity.**

She launched her brand. She bought followers. Her routine included daily posts, studying algorithms, and hustling harder than anyone. However, **as her platform grew, her passion faded.** She felt exhausted and empty, and she wondered why 'success' did not fulfil her.

One night after a sold-out event, Lara sat alone in her hotel room. She had achieved it. Yet inside, she felt numb—no joy, no peace, no connection to the God who had given her the gift of speech.

She realised something crucial: she had utilised her gift, but something had severed her from its divine origin. She pursued her desires instead of a holy calling.

Destiny's Path: The Story of Elijah

Now let's talk about Elijah, not the prophet, but a young man I met during a leadership retreat.

Elijah had a full scholarship to study engineering. He was brilliant, analytical, and deeply respected by his peers. However, in his second year, something changed. During a routine outreach programme, he felt an overwhelming sense of responsibility to help orphans and street children. It wasn't glamorous, and it certainly wasn't on his career plan. But he couldn't ignore the pull.

Everyone thought he was crazy. His parents were furious. "You're throwing your future away," they say. "You'll never make money doing that."

But Elijah **knew what he felt was not just a feeling; it was a calling**.

He finished school but spent his weekends building a shelter in the slums. It was hard. Money was tight. On many days, *he would feed the children and then go home hungry*. But he had never felt so alive.

Years later, someone transformed that same shelter into a foundation that educated hundreds of children and uplifted an entire community. Elijah never became wealthy, but he found fulfilment. He became a man who followed his divine calling rather than his comfort.

What is the difference between Calling and Desire?

Here's how you can tell:

Destiny Comes from a Higher Calling

- God or a higher force placed destiny in you.
- It is **not always what you initially want**; it often chooses you rather than the other way around.
- Destiny aligns with your natural talents, experiences, and a profound sense of **purpose**.

Ambition stems from personal drive

- **Your desires, society, culture, and competition shape ambition.**
- External factors often influence it (seeing others succeed, financial goals, fame).

- One can pursue ambition without considering purpose or impact.

Divine Calling	Personal Desire
Comes from God's heart	Comes from your own will
Feels like a burden you *must* carry	Feels like a goal you *want* to reach
Affects others and carries eternal value	Primarily benefits you
Often uncomfortable, stretching, and hard	Typically self-gratifying and safe
Leads to lasting fulfilment	May lead to short-term satisfaction but long-term emptiness

Desire says, *"I want to be successful."*

Calling says, "They are making me serve here, even if it costs me."

The Weight of Calling

A divine calling doesn't always seem "successful." It often appears to be the opposite.

You may face:

- **Rejection from people who don't understand.**
- **Delayed progress that challenges your faith.**
- **Loneliness because your path is so unique.**
- **Sacrifices others will never notice.**

But here's the truth: God will always equip you for what He calls you to do. And unlike personal desire, which fades when it gets tough, divine calling grants you a supernatural strength to endure pain with purpose.

Jesus: The Ultimate Example

Even Jesus experienced a moment where He could have chosen comfort over His calling. In the Garden of Gethsemane, aware of the suffering that awaited Him, He prayed:

"Father, if it is possible, let this cup pass from me. Yet not my will, but Yours be done."

Matthew 26:39

This reflects the tension between desire and destiny, the simple route and the one that feels good, versus what is genuinely good. Jesus opted for the path of suffering because it was in line with his purpose.

What Are the Signs That You Are Called to a Great Destiny?

Some individuals feel lost in life, unsure if they have an important purpose. However, some signs suggest you are destined for something greater.

1. **One feels a deep inner calling.**

2. **You face more challenges than others.** The bigger the calling, the greater the challenges.

3. **You Can't Ignore It**
   No matter how hard you try to resist, you feel drawn to a particular path. Destiny has a way of calling you back, even when you try to run from it.

4. **You Feel Unfulfilled in the Wrong Places. If you're engaged in something that isn't aligned with your destiny, you'll constantly feel restless, unsatisfied, and incomplete.**

   Example: Many successful individuals who chase wealth, fame, or status often feel empty because they are not fulfilling their true purpose.

How to Discern a Divine Calling in Your Life

If you're wondering whether what you're pursuing is your calling or just a personal desire, ask yourself:

1. **Does this align with God's values and purpose?**
2. **Would I still do it if no one applauded or paid me?**
3. **Do I feel burdened by this in a way that won't leave me alone?**

4. Does it help others and make a lasting impact?
5. Am I willing to endure discomfort for this cause?

If your answer is yes, you're likely walking in your divine calling.

Choose a Source That Lasts

- Your gift may get you noticed, but only your **calling will sustain you.**
- Ambition may make you wealthy, but only **purpose will make you whole.**
- Desire may excite you today, but only **destiny will fulfil you tomorrow.**

Lara chased her dream and found emptiness. Elijah followed his calling and found fulfilment. What will your story be?

Reflection Journal:

1. Have I been chasing personal ambition at the expense of my divine calling?
2. Is there a burden on my heart I've been neglecting because it seems inconvenient?
3. Am I willing to trust God with a purpose that may not always look "successful" in the world's eyes?

Your calling may involve pain, **but it also brings power, purpose, and peace.**

Now, ask yourself honestly: '**Am I building a life on my desires, or God's design?**'

God will always equip
you for what He calls
you to do.

Chapter 2

THE PURPOSE OF PAIN IN DESTINY

Pain as a Teacher and Refiner

"He knows the way that I take; when He has tested me, I will come forth as gold."

Job 23:10

Let's be honest, if you're holding this book right now, there's a high chance you've been through something painful. Maybe you're going through it right now.

This could be the sting of betrayal, a dream that didn't work out, rejection that still echoes in your soul or perhaps, it's that silent pain, the one no one else sees but that weighs heavily on your chest every night.

If so, I want you to know this: you are not alone. And more importantly, your pain is not pointless.

The Story of Kate: Pain in Real Time

Let me tell you a story about a woman named Kate. She is neither a celebrity nor a historical figure. Full of dreams, she was also passionate and talented. She was a natural encourager. From a young age, she was the one her friends turned to for advice and comfort. She knew she was called to help people, perhaps through coaching, ministry, or simply listening. It was her sweet spot.

But life hit her hard. Her first child died after birth. Her marriage fell apart. She lost her job in the same year her mother died of cancer. It felt as if life was trying to bury her.

"I thought I had a calling," she tells me once, tears in her eyes. "Now, I don't even know who I am anymore."

But what Kate didn't realise was that pain wasn't trying to destroy her. She was trying to uncover her destiny.

Pain Is a Refiner – Not a Punishment

> "See, I have refined you, though not as silver; I have tested you in the furnace of affliction."
> Isaiah 48:10

Let's start with the common falsehood many accept. Countless individuals facing difficult times in silence ask themselves:

- Did I do something wrong?
- Is God punishing me?
- Why does my life feel so much harder than everyone else's?

These thoughts are often whispered in private moments, during sleepless nights, tearful drives, or silent prayers. If you've ever felt this way, hear this clearly:

'Pain is not always punishment. Sometimes, it is a refinement.'

God did not mean for pain to destroy you. It's intended to **develop you.**

A Goldsmith's Story – From Heat to Glory

Let me take you into the workshop of a traditional goldsmith. He places a piece of raw gold — dusty, ugly, unrecognisable — into the fire. The temperature is high enough to burn away impurities. But the goldsmith observes. He knows if he leaves it in too long, it may get damaged. If he takes it out too early, it won't be pure. So he waits... until he can see his reflection in the gold. That's when he knows it's ready. That's precisely what God does with us.

When we go through painful seasons, it's not because He's angry. It's because He's refining us, burning away fear, pride, selfishness, and insecurity, until He can see His image in us.

This is what refinement looks like:

- You lose friendships so that you can learn discernment.
- Your job falls through, enabling you to find your true calling.
- Someone passes you over so that you can develop humility.
- You're misunderstood, so you stop living for validation.
- You hit rock bottom, so your foundation becomes unshakable.

What feels like loss is often the fire within you. You're not being destroyed; you're being **defined**. **God Does His Best Work in the Fire.** Some of the most transformative moments in the Bible occurred amid fire.

Let's examine the story in Daniel 3 of the three Hebrew boys (Shadrach, Meshach, and Abednego) who King Nebuchadnezzar's officials threw literally into a furnace because they refused to worship a false god. What seemed like punishment became an opportunity for God's power to manifest itself.

When the king looked in, he didn't just see the three of them; he saw a **fourth man**, the Son of God, walking in the fire with them.

> *The fire didn't consume them. It revealed who was strolling beside them.*

What if the pain you're experiencing right now is merely a prelude to a divine encounter?

The purpose of the fire is not just survival —it's transformation

Pain has the power to either harden your heart or soften it into gold. It can make you bitter or make you **better**. And here's what makes the difference: **'Your Perspective.'**

When you see pain as punishment, you resist it. When you view pain as a refinement, you **lean into it**, trusting that something is being formed within you.

Most people in a tough season are simply trying to **get through it**. Understandably so, pain is overwhelming, it feels unfair, and it can also feel like the very breath is being squeezed out of your life. So you grit your teeth, say your prayers, and hope to make it through.

But what if I told you that survival is not the aim? God didn't bring you into the fire just to help you crawl out the same. He brought you into it to transform you radically, profoundly, and permanently.

Survival says, "I just want this to end." Transformation says, "God, change me while I'm here." Survival is temporary. Transformation is eternal. You can survive something and still walk away bitter, afraid, or unchanged.

Transformation simply means:

- You don't simply go through the fire; you grow through it.
- You emerge wiser, not merely older.
- You become more profound, not just more resilient.

- You draw nearer to God, not further away.

This is the fire's ultimate assignment: **to make you who you could never become in comfort.**

The caterpillar doesn't just survive the cocoon—it becomes a butterfly.

Let's think about nature for a moment.

When a caterpillar enters the cocoon, it dissolves into a liquid. It becomes unrecognisable, even to itself. It undergoes a complete breakdown of form. If we were to take a peek halfway through and judge by appearance, we'd say it's dead, hopeless, and finished.

But that's the process of transformation. It doesn't appear attractive, but it often feels chaotic, painful, and isolating. Guess what? Something miraculous is happening inside. Wings are forming, identity is shifting, and a new creation is emerging. When the butterfly finally breaks free from the cocoon, it doesn't just fly. It flies because something transformed it.

Your fire is your cocoon. It's not meant to destroy you; it's intended to reshape you. That breakdown? It's making space for a new vision. That heartbreak? It's teaching you what true love demands. That job loss? It's breaking the illusion of stability so you can find purpose. That season of silence? It's helping you hear God's voice clearly without the noise.

Transformation doesn't occur when you flee the fire. It happens when you permit the fire to transform you.

Biblical Transformation in the Fire

Let's revisit Shadrach, Meshach, and Abednego (Daniel 3). They were thrown into a furnace for refusing to bow to a false god. When the king looked into the fire, he saw not three men, but four. The fourth was like the Son of God.

When the men came out, here's what Scripture says: their bodies were unharmed. Their clothes were unscathed, and they didn't even smell like smoke.

But here's the best part: **the only thing that was burned off them was the ropes that bound them.** Let that sink in:

The fire didn't touch their skin—but it destroyed their bondage.

That's transformation. You go in tied up. You come out **free**. *Transformation always leaves a mark, but not a wound.* When the fire has truly transformed you:

- You speak with more authority, but less ego.
- You carry confidence, but not pride.
- You discern quickly, but judge slowly.
- You forgive more easily but tolerate less nonsense.
- You walk in peace but fight for your purpose.

People won't always understand the new you, but that's okay. You didn't go through the fire to be **liked**. You went through to be **reborn**.

'The Real You Is in the Fire,'

The version of you that's bold, healed, and deeply rooted in purpose? That version is in the fire, waiting to emerge. That version is being forged in the flames.

The leader, the servant, the warrior, the light bearer? They're all within the fire, concealed beneath the ashes of your former self. God is not summoning you simply to endure the fire. He's calling you to transform yourself through the fire so you can receive what follows.

Your Fire is Your Formation Ground.

You don't come out of the fire empty-handed. You come out:

- Carrying wisdom that books can't teach
- Walking in the power that pain has generated
- Radiating glory that only pressure could unlock

And when you emerge, don't just say, "I survived." But declare, **"I'm not who I was. My strength has increased. I'm freer. I'm transformed."**

Personal Reflection: My Refining Season

Let me get personal. There was a time in my life when everything I had built seemed to fall apart all at once. The betrayal I didn't see coming, the opportunity I prayed for that slipped through my fingers, and the silence from God that made me question everything.

For months, I asked God, *"Why me?"* But eventually, the question changed. It became, *"What are you building in me through this?"* That season stripped me of pride, purified my intentions, and matured my character. It forced me to let go of the image and embrace **integrity**. My platform was transformed into a ministry through it. It turned my pain into a message. Would I want to go through it again? No way. But am I grateful I did? **Absolutely.**

How to Recognise the Refining Fire.

Here are signs you're going through a refining season:

- You feel stretched beyond your comfort zone.
- Old habits, relationships, or patterns are being exposed.
- You feel isolated, like God is stripping things away.
- You're forced to confront parts of yourself you've ignored.
- Your character is being tested more than your talent.

What to Do When You're in a Fire

Pain has a way of making us panic, question everything, and want out. But the intention of the refining fire isn't to consume you; here is how to posture your heart and mind when you find yourself in that season.

1. **Surrender; don't resist**

   Stop asking, "Why me?" Instead, ask, "What now, God?" It's natural to ask, "Why me?" during times of suffering. We all do. But that question often keeps us trapped in pain instead of learning from it. Surrender doesn't mean giving up; it means giving in. It involves choosing to trust God with what you don't understand.

   What surrender looks like:

   - Laying down your expectations of how things should be.
   - Releasing control of timelines and outcomes.
   - Allowing God to utilise suffering to mould you, instead of resenting Him for it.

   Change your prayer from asking God to remove you from this situation to asking God to help you grow because of it. You'll discover that peace doesn't come when the fire ends, but it comes when you stop fighting it and start flowing with God in it.

2. Stay in the Process

Don't escape the pain too quickly. The gold isn't ready until the process is complete. It's tempting to look for shortcuts, exits, or distractions. We want the pain to stop immediately. But like gold in a furnace, coming out too early leaves us incomplete. If God is shaping your heart, don't rush it. Allow patience to do its perfect work. Let discomfort build depth. Let hardship increase humility.

By escaping prematurely, we find ourselves trapped in recurring cycles of pain. We miss out on valuable lessons and enter the next phase of our lives unprepared.

Staying in the process means:

- Remain prayerful even when you feel spiritually dry.
- Holding on to your faith when nothing seems to make sense.
- Choosing obedience, even when it is costly.

Remember: *The process is painful, but the product is powerful.*

3. Stay Close to God's Presence

The fire may feel lonely, but you are never alone.

Like the Hebrew boys in Daniel 3, God doesn't always rescue you immediately from the fire. Sometimes, he joins you in it. His presence itself is the miracle. Even in the fire, He is there — not watching from afar but walking with you.

How do you stay close whilst in the fire?

- **Worship even when you don't feel like it** – praise can shift your perspective.
- **Stay in the Word** – Scripture becomes a lifeline when your emotions betray you.
- **Journal your prayers** – it reminds you God is listening, even in silence.
- **Surround yourself with people of faith – their strength can support you when yours wanes.**

The fire reveals who God is in ways our comfort never could. Don't run from Him; run to Him.

4. Let Go of What's Being Burned Away

Sometimes, the pain we experience is not just caused by the heat but also by the loss of things we've become attached to, such as relationships, roles, old habits, outdated identities, and false beliefs about ourselves.

'If it's dying in the fire, it's not meant for your future. Let it go.'

The refining fire removes what cannot accompany you into your next season. However, the longer we hold on, the more painful the burn becomes. You may mourn something God is mercifully removing.

Letting go means releasing toxic relationships with no need for closure, abandoning the version of success you once idolised, and saying farewell to your comfort zone so you can grow.

The fire isn't just shaping you; it's destroying your reliance on what no longer benefits your purpose. *Say this with me:* **"God, I trust You with what You're taking. Even when it hurts, I trust you're making room for what's better."**

Every fire has a purpose. You can come out bitter or brilliantly transformed. The key is how you respond during it. You don't need to be perfect or feel strong every day; simply stay surrendered, present, and open to what God is doing. One day, you'll look in the mirror and see someone you didn't recognise before: refined, focused, prepared, and glowing with purpose.

When You Emerge, You will Shine.

The refining process isn't endless. One day, you'll emerge on the other side, feeling stronger, wiser, humbler, and purer. Looking back, you'll realise: The fire didn't kill me. It revealed the gold within.

God doesn't waste pain; He uses it to refine purpose, and when He's finished, you won't just survive the fire—you'll emerge shining with glory.

Destructive Pain vs. Transformative Pain

Not all pain serves the same purpose. Some pain destroys, while some should transform. The key is learning the difference and how to respond.

Destructive Pain:

- Comes from staying in cycles that God has told you to leave
- Involves compromise, disobedience, or misplaced identity
- Leaves you bitter, stuck, or ashamed
- Feels like it's draining your purpose, not developing it

Example: Remaining in a toxic relationship that God has explicitly instructed you to leave, but fear or pride keeps you there. The longer you stay, the more the pain pulls you away from who God created you to be.

Transformative Pain:

- Comes as part of your refining process
- It's not caused by sin, but by growth
- It pushes you toward purpose and maturity
- Feels crushing, but in hindsight, it was the making of you

An example is Joseph in the Bible. His brothers betrayed him, threw him in a pit, sold him into slavery, and imprisoned him for something he didn't do. But each level of pain led him closer to his divine position. When his time came, he was ready, because pain had prepared him.

Let's take a step back and observe the bigger picture of destiny. Greatness always accompanies deep pain. Let's consider briefly the lessons from historical figures.

Joseph (Genesis 37–50)

His dream was divine, but it did not come easily. **Before the palace was the pit, before honour was humiliation, and before leadership was loneliness.** But by the end of his story, he said something so powerful to his brothers who betrayed him:

> "You meant it for evil, but God meant it for good—to bring about this present result."

Joseph understood the secret: Pain was part of the purpose.

Nelson Mandela

27 years in prison. Years of abuse, silence, and stolen time. But what emerged? A man shaped by pain, not broken by it. He didn't come out bitter; he came out ready to lead a nation. Pain prepared him for global influence.

Jesus Christ

He was God, yet suffered. He felt every betrayal, every lash, every rejection. Why? Pain was the path to our salvation. Without the cross, there would be no resurrection. Without death, there is no life, and without Gethsemane, there is no glory.

His story shows us you don't escape destiny by avoiding pain; you fulfil it by enduring it.

What About You? Maybe you're in your own "pit season" right now. You may ask, *Why me? What did I do wrong? How long will this last?* Friend, take a deep breath and look deeper. Pain is not your punishment; it might just be your preparation. You're not being buried; you're being planted. And when the time is right, you will bloom with power, with purpose, and with perspective.

Reflective Journal: What Is Pain Teaching You?

Here are some questions to consider during your quiet time:

1. What pain am I currently experiencing, and how have I been interpreting it?

2. Am I running from pain or allowing God to use it to refine me?
3. Is this pain destructive or transformative? What is it pushing me to become?
4. What has pain revealed in me that I didn't know was there?

Don't Waste the Pain

The greatest tragedy is not pain; it's wasted pain. Pain that doesn't grow you. Pain that you ignore, resent, or pretend isn't there. But when you lean into it, listen to it, and let God lead you through it, pain becomes the catalyst for purpose.

Like Kate, you may feel overwhelmed right now, but years from now, you'll look back and say, *"That season didn't kill me. It revealed me."* Your pain is part of the story. Don't give up now. You're being refined.

You don't need to be perfect or feel strong every day; simply stay surrendered, present, and open to what God is doing.

PART TWO

The Pains That Shape Destiny

Chapter 3

THE PAIN OF REJECTION AND BETRAYAL

"He was despised and rejected by men, a man of sorrows and acquainted with grief…"

Isaiah 53:3

Why Rejection Is a Sign of Redirection

Let's begin with a truth few care to face: rejection hurts; betrayal destroys. They are two of the most painful experiences for the human soul because they strike at the very core of our identity.

They originate from those we trusted, invested in, and shared our hearts with. When they leave or betray us, we question, Was I not enough? How could they do this? Or what did I do to deserve it? I've experienced this, and I know it doesn't just hurt; it shatters you.

The Story of Nia: Rejected but Redirected

I had the chance to speak with a lady called Nia during one of my coaching sessions. Nia had been best friends with Tasha since they were in school. Their friendship felt like family. They started different businesses together, prayed together, and travelled together. Nia shared her dreams, secrets, and fears.

One day, Tasha secured a significant contract that she scheduled to work on with Nia, and suddenly, she ghosted her. Nia was stunned; there was no explanation, no closure, just silence.

A few weeks later, she discovered Tasha had accepted the deal without consulting her and had informed others that Nia "wasn't ready for the opportunity." It wasn't just betrayal; it was a ripping apart of the soul ties.

Nia cried for weeks. She questioned everything about herself. Until one night, in tears, she whispers, "God, if you allowed this, then show me the purpose."

Months went by, and Nia retreated inward. During this period, she dedicated herself to healing and reorganisation, taking essential steps to reconstruct her life. This process of self-discovery helped her become stronger, wiser, and more discerning.

As she delved more deeply into her thoughts and feelings, Nia released the burdens of her past. She learned to trust herself more, recognising that genuine growth often emerges from moments of solitude. It wasn't easy, but each challenge helped her approach her destined self.

With newfound clarity, Nia pursued her ambitions with renewed purpose. She realised that the journey ahead would not always be straightforward, but she felt prepared to face any obstacles in her way. She embraced her independence, discovering strength in her solitude and confidence in her choices.

As she began rebuilding, brick by brick, she visualised a future that reflected her true self—a life filled with intention, passion, and resilience. The pain she once endured no longer felt like a burden but a vital part of her story that had prepared her for greatness. Nia was ready to step into her destiny, no longer afraid of the challenges that came with it. And a year later, she signed a bigger deal than the one she lost, with people who respected her integrity.

Looking back, Nia realised that betrayal wasn't her end — it was her redirection.

You see, what seems to be rejection is often a divine intervention. God will use rejection to:

- **Protect you** from people who can't go where He's taking you.
- **Redirect you** from paths that look good but aren't God.
- **Expose hearts** that don't belong in your inner circle.

Sometimes it's not that they stopped loving you; it's that they never truly could bear the weight of your destiny. And so, in His mercy, God allows rejection not to punish you, but to position you.

Joseph's Story: Rejected by Blood, Elevated by God

Joseph had a divine dream. But his brothers, jealous and threatened, sold him into slavery. Can you imagine that pain? His blood rejected him, and those he would have died for betrayed him.

And yet, that rejection was precisely what propelled him towards his destiny.

If they hadn't sold him, he wouldn't have ended up in Egypt. He wouldn't have entered Pharaoh's house if he hadn't gone to Egypt. If he hadn't reached Pharaoh, he wouldn't have saved a nation. What they intended for evil, God used for good.

There's no sugarcoating it: betrayal breaks your heart. It's one thing to be wounded by life; it's another to be hurt by love. Jesus himself knew this pain. A stranger didn't betray him; Judas betrayed him, someone he walked with, ate with, and loved.

But what's truly powerful is this: Jesus knew Judas would betray Him, and yet He still washed his feet. Why? Because Jesus never allowed someone else's betrayal to change His identity or character. He stayed gentle. His focus remained steady. He kept his purpose intact. And that's the key for you too.

Betrayal doesn't just break your heart—it shakes your foundation. It makes you question who you can trust, whether you ever saw the person clearly, and sometimes, whether you can trust **your judgement again.**

The journey to heal from betrayal isn't quick, and it's not straightforward. But healing is achievable—and it begins with deciding to open your heart.

Let's walk through the steps—gently, but with honesty.

How to Begin Healing from Betrayal

1. **Acknowledge the Pain – Don't Pretend It Didn't Hurt**

    The first step towards healing is allowing yourself to feel. Betrayal is not something to dismiss lightly. It's not something to just "move on" from. It needs to be experienced, confronted, and acknowledged. Whether it was a spouse, a friend, a mentor, a sibling, or someone you trusted deeply, recognise that what happened hurt you.

    Cry if you need to. Say it out loud: *"That hurt me."* Journal what it made you feel—rejected, devalued, blindsided, disrespected. You cannot heal what you pretend doesn't exist. **Truth is the starting point of transformation.**

2. **Grieve the Loss – Even Toxic People Leave Holes**

    This is the step we often overlook: grief. But healing requires mourning, not only for the person but also for what you believed the relationship to be.

Sometimes we mourn the version of the person we hoped was real, the future we pictured with them, and the emotional investment, time, and memories we can't retrieve. Even if the person wasn't good for you, they occupied a place in your life. Their betrayal left a void.

And it's okay to grieve for that. Grief doesn't mean you want them back; it means you're honouring what you lost and making space for what's coming next.

Let the tears fall, sit in silence, talk it out with a trusted voice and let God meet you in that grief, because **He weeps with you.**

3. **Don't internalise the betrayal. Their actions reveal who they are, not you.**

One of betrayal's worst tricks is convincing you it's your fault. But here's the truth: how someone treats you reflects their character, not your worth.

If someone lied, manipulated, abandoned, or deceived you, it doesn't mean you are flawed. It reveals their dishonesty. Betrayal is their wound reflected onto you; don't let it shape your identity.

You are still:
1. Worthy of love
2. Deserving of loyalty
3. Capable of discernment

Healing starts when you detach your identity from their actions.

4. **Let God vindicate you – you do not need revenge. You need rest.**

> *"The Lord will fight for you; you need only to be still."*
> Exodus 14:14

After a betrayal, the urge to *"set the record straight," "make them pay,"* or *"tell your side"* is natural. But revenge destroys your peace, and it keeps your soul tied to the very person you're trying to escape from.

God never asks you to vindicate yourself; He says, "*Be still.*" Let **him** handle it. And he will.

When you let God fight your battles:

- He restores what you lost in ways you couldn't imagine.
- He shields your heart and elevates you beyond the drama.
- He provides exposure, elevation, and peace at the moment.

Rest doesn't mean doing nothing. It means **choosing trust over retaliation**. Don't waste energy chasing justice. Let the God of justice handle it while you heal.

5. Choose Forgiveness—For *Your* Freedom

> "*Forgive us our trespasses, as we forgive those who trespass against us...*"
>
> Matthew 6:12

Forgiveness doesn't mean that what happened was acceptable; it doesn't mean you welcome them back into your life. **It means you are letting go of their hold on your soul.**

Unforgiveness is a prison. You think you're punishing them, but you're keeping yourself bound to pain. Holding on to offence can pollute your peace, block your blessings or even harden your heart. Forgiveness is not a feeling; it's a daily decision and sometimes an hourly one.

Say this out loud: *"I forgive them, not because they deserve it, but because I deserve peace."*

Forgiveness breaks the chain, and it hands the wound over to God. It says, *"You don't get to live in my head or heart anymore."*

Betrayal can temporarily break you, but it doesn't have to define you forever. Yes, it hurts, and yes, it changes you. But if you choose to heal over hatred and wholeness over revenge, you will rise with;

- Clearer discernment
- A guarded, but open heart
- Deeper wisdom
- And a peace that no person can steal

You might never receive the apology, nor hear the truth, but you can walk away whole. **Because your healing is not in their hands—it's in God's.**

Learning Discernment Through Pain

Rejection and betrayal teach you lessons that discernment alone cannot, making you focus on tone, not just words; consistency, not just charisma; fruit, not just potential; and peace in your spirit, not just excitement in your emotions.

You will become wiser without losing your gentle nature. You will learn to love others without revealing your soul on a platter, and you will offer access based on character, not merely connection. And that, my friend, is a powerful place to be.

Perhaps your rejection originated from a parent who never loved you as you needed, or from a friend who knew your scars and used them against you. It could also have come from a partner who promised to be forever but walked away when things became difficult.

Let me say this with love and passion:

- Even though they walked away, your destiny remained.
- Even though they left, God stayed.
- They closed a door, but God's redirection will reveal the one you were always meant to walk through.

Let it hurt, let it heal, but **don't let it stop you.**

Your task is too important to be dismissed by those who cannot recognise your value.

Reflection Journal

1. Who rejected or betrayed me, and what wound did it leave?
2. Have I been holding on to bitterness, or have I honestly released it?
3. What did I learn about myself and others through this pain?
4. Is God using this rejection to redirect me to something higher?
5. What boundaries do I now need to build with wisdom and discernment?

Note:

You are not alone in your heartbreak. Even though someone betrayed Jesus, Joseph faced rejection. Even you, chosen, called, gifted, will face it, but don't let rejection define your worth. Let it **refine your direction.** You may cry now, but you'll **rise wiser, stronger, more anointed** because every heartbreak is a step closer to **who you are.**

Chapter 4

THE PAIN OF LONELINESS ON THE JOURNEY

When It Feels Like You're the Only One Walking This Path

"Then Jesus was led by the Spirit into the wilderness…"

Matthew 4:1

The Ache No One Talks About

There's a kind of pain that creeps in silently and settles deep. It doesn't knock you over like betrayal. A loud bang doesn't accompany loss when it happens. It just lingers quietly, like a shadow you can't shake.

That pain is loneliness.

The pain of loneliness is one of the most overlooked struggles on the way to purpose. It's not the loud pain. It's not the sort that earns sympathy. There are no visible wounds. No one brings flowers or checks in when you're hurting because, from the outside, everything looks "fine."

But inside, it aches.

And if you've ever gone through a time when your phone went silent, your circle grew smaller, your bed felt colder, and your prayers sounded like echoes, you understand precisely what I mean. It's the pain that quietly sneaks in late at night. It's like achieving something when you have nobody to share it with. When you want to open your heart to someone, but the space where trust once was feels empty. When people surround you, yet you feel utterly invisible.

Yes, loneliness runs deep, especially when you're called.

It's the pain of being surrounded but unseen, the pain of being known but not understood, and the pain of moving towards something great while feeling completely alone.

Why Destiny Often Feels So Isolating

People often overlook that the path to destiny is not only steep but also narrow, and such paths do not accommodate many travellers. Many of history's most anointed, impactful, and world-changing figures first experienced periods of solitude. This was not because of flaws or neglect, but because God was working within them in ways that couldn't occur amidst the chaos of community life.

There is something sacred about being unseen.

Think about Moses; before facing Pharaoh, he spent forty years in the desert. Just him, sheep, and silence. There, he learned how to lead, how to listen, and, most importantly, how to trust God alone.

The Spirit led Jesus into the wilderness before he healed the sick and preached to multitudes. The Son of God. Called. Chosen. Sent. Alone.

This reveals an important truth: God often does His most extraordinary work in solitude, not to punish us, but to prepare us.

The Silent Room

Faye was a vivacious woman who could light up any room with her presence. People considered her a reliable friend—sending encouraging texts, making others laugh, and remembering everyone's birthdays.

Also, she embodied the dreamer and knew she was meant for something greater. When she courageously left her job to follow her calling full-time, she expected excitement and encouragement. She believed her friends and family would cheer her on, support her, and walk alongside her. Instead, they became silent.

Initially, the changes were subtle- calls dwindled, texts shortened, and invitations ceased. She convinced herself they were simply busy. However, the actual pain came during the moments she had no one to reach out to. She celebrated a major victory alone in her flat, eating generic cake. When she got sick, she realised no one was aware. And when she debuted her first product, the people she had supported didn't even attend.

She remembers sitting on her floor one evening, crying more than she ever had before. Not because she regretted her decision, but because she never expected that pursuing her purpose would feel so... lonely.

"God," she whispers, "did I do something wrong? Why would you call me into something that makes me feel this alone?"

And then, in that quiet, with mascara-streaked cheeks and a tired heart, she felt God say:

"I didn't call you to be alone. I called you to me."

Why Destiny Often Requires Solitude

Faye's story resonates with many. When God calls you forward, He often calls others away—not because they are evil, but because they belong to your past chapter, not your future.

We believe that walking into purpose means walking with a crowd, but in Scripture and life, we see the opposite.

- Moses was alone in the desert.
- David was alone in the fields.
- Joseph was alone in prison.
- Jesus was alone in the wilderness.

Not because anyone forgot them, but because God was doing something sacred in their solitude. He was stripping away the noise, the craving for approval, and the crutches. He was teaching them to walk not by popularity but by faith, not with company but with conviction.

The Emotional Journey of Loneliness

Loneliness doesn't come suddenly. It slowly seeps in, little by little.

At first, you feel forgotten. And it feels like your presence no longer matters. Then comes the resentment. You remember all the times you showed up for others, and wonder why they didn't show up for you. Then comes the shame. You wonder if something's wrong with you. *Am I too much? Too different? Not worthy of love?*

It's a dark spiral, a silent one.

You walk through your day, show up at work, post something positive, maybe even smile at church. But behind it all, there's a quiet ache that says, *"I just want someone to see me. To sit with me. To understand me."*

But here's what most people miss: Loneliness, though painful, can become holy.

Loneliness is not isolation—it's an invitation

There's a difference between being alone and being isolated.

Isolation occurs when you withdraw from the world because of fear, shame, or self-protection. That's when you stop letting anyone in and convince yourself you don't need others at all. It can lead to depression, bitterness, and despair, cutting you off from both people and God. This is dangerous because while God uses solitude to build you, the enemy exploits isolation to break you.

Loneliness is something that can happen to you, especially during times of transition. It's a natural part of being called to a deeper place. When surrendered, loneliness can become a sacred space. A space where you rediscover who you are away from the noise of others. It's a space where God becomes more than just a concept; He becomes your Companion. It's a space where silence becomes your sanctuary, and stillness becomes your strength.

That's what happened to Faye.

In her loneliness, she resumed writing, not for an audience, but for herself. From a raw and honest place, she began praying, not with elaborate words.

Long walks were her habit, and she cried openly. She journaled about her pain. She listened to worship music and allowed it to wash over her. And gradually, day by day, the ache shifted; the emptiness transformed into openness. The silence became sacred, and the loneliness developed into intimacy with God.

The Loneliness That Comes with Growth

No one warns you that growth can cost you your company. As you pursue your purpose, you'll notice some friendships no longer feel right. You'll outgrow conversations, spaces, and even people you once felt at home with. And it's painful, not because they are bad people, but because you're changing. You're being drawn upward. And not everyone can climb with you.

Initially, you'll try to hold on by texting more and explaining yourself to keep the peace. However, the more you cling to what God is working to separate you from, the greater inner tension you'll feel in your spirit.

And eventually, you'll face a choice: their comfort or your calling.

That's when the loneliness hits the hardest.

If you're in a lonely season, don't shut your heart to others. Allow God to do the deep work and speak to you without the noise of everyone else's opinions. However, remember that you were never supposed to face life entirely alone. When the right people arrive, welcome them in.

When the Quiet Feels Too Loud

I recall a time in my life when I felt utterly alone. Everything was changing. The friendships I had relied on for years faded. I left the church where I was serving as a choir leader and was content to leave everything behind when I moved to another church. I felt lonely there, but I loved their music, and it became a source of comfort to me. It was five years of loneliness. It was painful inside.

Though I intended to return, I found myself unable. I remained in prayer daily, allowing God to be present with me. I was stepping into a new version of myself, and it terrified me.

There were nights I cried out to God, "Why would You give me this dream, this calling, and then leave me to walk it alone?"

And softly, like a whisper, I heard Him speak: "I'm not leaving you. I'm leading you."

It didn't eliminate the pain, but it gave it meaning. Reflecting now, I understand what He was guiding me through. In the silence, I learned to listen for His voice. In loneliness, I discovered the feeling of being genuinely understood by someone. Without external applause, I learned to act with obedience rather than seeking approval.

That version of me — rooted, sure, unshaken: that's who the fire was forming all along.

Using Loneliness as a Catalyst for Growth

Rather than dulling the loneliness with noise, what if you embraced it?

Use this season to rediscover:
- Your voice, your dreams, your values
- Those parts of yourself that were lost in relationships and roles.
- People-pleasing hides away passions.
- Prayers that you stopped praying because life got too busy.

You see, loneliness isn't always the enemy; sometimes, it's the bridge to the deepest parts of yourself and the most authentic connection with God you'll ever experience.

So what do you do when you're on the lonely part of the journey? You lean in.

Begin listening to God, to your heart, and to the unspoken truths you've been too busy to confront. Reflect on who you are without the noise.

Heal the parts of you that need crowd validation to feel worthy.

Rediscover your voice, your values, and your vision. It won't always feel productive. But trust me, the deep, silent work happening in your soul right now is laying the foundation for the future you're praying for.

Solitude is where roots grow. And when storms come, they cannot easily shake anything with strong roots.

If You're Feeling Alone

This isn't the end of your story. It's the middle, and middles are always messy and uncertain. But they are also sacred. You may not have the friendships you once had, you might not have a cheering crowd, and you may not even feel understood, but don't confuse being hidden with being forgotten. Don't mistake a quiet season for a wasted one.

God carries out His deepest, most transformative work when no one is watching. When He's finished, you'll come out stronger, wiser, more discerning, and more grounded in who you are than ever before.

You won't just endure loneliness. You'll emerge from it—with clarity, courage, and conviction.

Reflective Journal

If you're walking through loneliness right now, here are some heart-level questions to sit with:

- Have I confused solitude with rejection?
- What is this quiet season revealing about who I am and what I truly need?
- Which part of me is God trying to strengthen without the noise of other people?

- Am I prepared to let go of old connections to make space for new, healthy ones?

Destiny never meant for you to stay hidden forever. But for now, if you're in a lonely place, breathe. You are not falling behind; you are in transition and formation.

Allow the quiet to do its work, let loneliness become a classroom, and trust that when the time is right, God will bring the right people, the right doors, and the right next steps.

For now, walk with Him. And let Him walk with you because, even when it feels like you're alone, you are never truly alone.

Begin listening to God, to your heart, and to the unspoken truths you've been too busy to confront.

Chapter 5

THE PAIN OF DELAY AND WAITING

When It Feels Like God Is Taking Too Long

"Hope deferred makes the heart sick, but a longing fulfilled is a tree of life."

Proverbs 13:12

The Pain No One Sees

There is a kind of pain that doesn't scream but suffocates. It's not the pain of a breakup nor the sting of betrayal. This is not a trauma of loss. It's quieter than all of those but often deeper.

It's the pain of waiting.

Each day, you wake up feeling a quiet ache. You do your best to stay hopeful, keep busy, and carry on. You go to church, serve, and pray, despite that, nothing changes. Time passes, and the doors remain shut.

People ask you, "Any updates?" and you smile while lying. You respond, "Not yet," but inwardly, you wonder, will it ever happen?

This is what waiting feels like: heavy, silent and exhausting.

And if you're not cautious, it can also become risky because it tempts you to abandon what you once believed.

When Waiting Feels Like Being Forgotten

One of the cruellest lies the enemy whispers during waiting seasons is this:

"If God loved you, He wouldn't make you wait."

You observe everyone progressing: your best friend got married, your co-worker got promoted, and even a stranger you met during a TikTok live shared their testimony. And you? Still praying, still hopeful, and still stuck. You wonder, 'What did I do wrong? Maybe I missed it. Maybe God changed His mind.'

But I need you to hear this with your whole heart:

"Delay does not mean denial."

God's timing is never late, never rushed, and never confused. If you're still in the waiting room, it's not because He's forgotten you, but because He's shaping something greater than you imagined.

Chim's Story: The Delay that Built Him

Chim always knew he would guide others through writing, speaking, and teaching. His dream ignited his passion. He attended conferences, started a blog, and volunteered at his local church.

But year after year, it seemed like nothing grew. His blog rarely received any views. He had ideas that were rejected, and his prayers for influence went unanswered. He watched others rise, even some who didn't appear as committed as he was, and he felt truly hidden, overlooked, and invisible.

One day, in a fit of frustration, he cries out: *"God, why not me? I'm trying so hard."*

In that moment, he felt something drop into him and a word that jumped to him, saying;

> *"I'm not building your platform. I'm building your roots."*

It broke him, but it also set him free.

He finally understood that God wasn't punishing him but protecting him. This realisation helped him develop into a version of himself that could handle his calling. During this waiting period, he grew deeper, wiser, more healed, and humbler. He stayed committed to his role, focusing on his task rather than seeking validation.

Years later, several doors opened for him, but he didn't rush through them as someone desperate for validation; he walked through them with grace.

Why Waiting Is Not Wasting

The world tells us that if we're not "there" yet, we're behind, but heaven doesn't operate on our calendar. With God, **time is a tool, not a threat**. He uses seasons of waiting not to harm you, but to **make you ready**.

God delays for reasons we often cannot see:

- To protect you from something you're not prepared to handle
- To grow your character so your gift doesn't destroy you

- To ensure people and circumstances are aligned in ways only He can
- To test your obedience and strengthen your trust

When you feel God is making you wait, remember that He is shaping you into someone new. The waiting period is active; it's not idle or passive. Instead, it's a sacred space where growth occurs.

What happens to you while you wait matters

Here's the harsh truth: not everyone who waits improves. Some grow bitter, angry, distrustful, and cynical. But those who give up waiting do not experience transformation.

Waiting produces:

- **Depth** – You seek God, not just His hand.
- **Discernment** – You learn to recognise divine timing.
- **Detachment** – You stop idolising outcomes and trust God's process.

- **Devotion** – You mature in faith and commitment.

The waiting isn't just about what you'll *get*. It's about who you'll *become*.

How to Manage Divine Delays

So, how do you keep walking when it feels like nothing is happening?

1. Stay present in your today

Don't delay your happiness by waiting for "one day." Start appreciating the life you're living now, even as you hope for more. God is present in the moment, not only in future breakthroughs.

2. Anchor Yourself in God's Word

When the delay lasts too long, your emotions may deceive you. Stay grounded in promises, not feelings. Write them down, say them aloud, and memorise them.

3. Talk Honestly with God

Don't pretend. God can handle your tears, frustration, and confusion. It is insignificant to say, "God, I'm tired." It's intimidating.

4. Celebrate Others While You Wait

The true sign of maturity is the ability to celebrate others' successes while anticipating your own. Celebrating with others reduces the urge to compare and helps keep your heart open.

5. Building Patience and Endurance

We often think of patience means sitting quietly. But biblical patience is powerful. The strength lies in maintaining belief even when the promise seems unfulfilled. It's endurance under pressure. It's trusting God's process even when you don't understand it.

Romans 5:4 states that suffering leads to endurance, endurance fosters character, and character breeds hope. Therefore, the delay doesn't destroy your hope. You won't just receive what you prayed for; you'll grow into someone strong enough to hold it.

If you are still waiting, please hear this:

- God has not forgotten you.
- Someone does not overlook you.
- Punishment is not happening to you.
- The process of preparing you is underway.

Right now, God is performing profound work within you that you cannot hurry. When the door opens, the relationship begins, or the breakthrough arrives, you won't step into it as someone desperate for validation.

Enter with confidence, thinking, 'I didn't arrive here by chance. I didn't push this forward alone. God planned it, and I'm ready.' Be patient, trust fully, and focus on Him instead of the clock. When it finally happens, you'll realise it wasn't a delay but a divine arrangement for something even better.

Reflection Journal

1. What have I believed about God during my waiting season?
2. Have I been dodging the process rather than 3. accepting it?
3. What growth or healing can I seek while I wait?
4. Do I trust that God's timing will be worth the wait?

Chapter 6

THE PAIN OF SACRIFICE AND LETTING GO

*Releasing What No Longer Fits
Where You're Going*

"Unless a grain of wheat falls to the ground and dies, it remains alone. But if it dies, it produces much fruit."

John 12:24

Letting go doesn't always look like a dramatic ending. Sometimes, it's the quiet, invisible kind, the kind where you slowly realise that something, or someone, you once loved, no longer fits. And even though you know it's time, it still tears you apart.

Letting go is one of the hardest things we do as humans. Not because we're weak but because we're loyal. We hold on to relationships, habits, environments, and mindsets, even when they're suffocating us, because we can't bear the thought of the space they'll leave behind. We keep trying to make something old work in a season God is trying to make new.

Judith had been with her childhood best friend, Cindi, for over 20 years. They had walked through everything together: school, heartbreaks, triumphs, and faith. They were inseparable. But over time, something shifted.

While Judith worked on discovering her purpose, healing from trauma, strengthening her faith, and embracing leadership, Cindi stayed trapped in cycles of gossip, bitterness, and petty thoughts. Whenever they met, Judith felt exhausted, as if she was being pulled back into an older version of herself that no longer existed. She tried to ignore these feelings, telling herself, "Maybe I'm changing too fast." Despite her efforts, she continued to feel drained until one day she heard a speaker say:

Some people should be part of your history, but not your destiny.

The words shattered her, and she wept for days — not out of anger, but grief. How do you say farewell to someone who never hurt you, but also cannot walk with you into the next chapter? How do you explain to someone that your heart is shifting and you're not better than them, but you're becoming someone they won't understand?

Letting go isn't always about loss. Sometimes it's about honouring the part they played and releasing them before resentment develops.

What Are You Willing to Give Up for Destiny?

Destiny will demand from you. It won't just require your passion; it will also need your choices. It will call on you for comfort, convenience, and sometimes, companionship. You cannot carry everything into your future. You cannot hold on to purpose in one hand and cling to burdens in the other.

Many people get stuck here. They sense the push towards something greater but hesitate to let go of the familiar. As a result, they remain in dead-end relationships, toxic patterns, limited thinking, and roles they've outgrown. They also cling to versions of themselves that no longer serve who they are becoming. The tragedy is that they settle for what's safe when they are called to what's sacred.

Destiny will ask you questions such as

- Would you be willing to walk alone for a while?
- Would you accept the possibility of being misunderstood?
- Will you grieve the old to give birth to the new?

You *can't rise and cling at the same time.*

The Cost of Growth: Relationships, Comfort, and Old Mindsets

Growth feels rewarding when we share our achievements and milestones, but genuine growth

— the kind that occurs behind closed doors — often brings about deep discomfort. It entails letting go of relationships with people who can no longer see your true self, creating a silence where validation once thrived.

This journey forces us to be honest with ourselves about habits that may give temporary pleasure but ultimately keep us stuck. It asks us to confront thoughts that feel familiar but come from fear and self-doubt. Embracing this personal growth is challenging, yet it is through this struggle that we find the strength to change and progress. Proper growth is messy, painful, and deeply personal, but it is also where we discover our true potential.

Sometimes, growth means realising that:

- Your tendency to please others comes from childhood survival. You learned early on that approval from others often felt essential for safety and acceptance, influencing how you approach relationships today.

- Your hustle comes from feeling unworthy. Possibly, the constant urge to succeed and prove yourself arises from a belief that your achievements connect to your self-worth, rather than your inherent value.

- Your relationship was based on fear rather than love. Many of these connections may have stemmed from insecurity and the desire for validation instead of genuine affection and mutual respect.

- Your "confidence" was a mask for insecurity. The bravado you displayed to the world might have been a way to shield your vulnerabilities, concealing the self-doubt that remained beneath the surface.

Recognising these truths is a vital step toward healing and genuine growth. It encourages you to re-evaluate your motivations and adopt healthier patterns that better reflect your true self.

God will confront all of that, not to shame you, but to set you free. Yet, freedom doesn't start with arriving. It begins with letting go.

How to Embrace the Pain of Transformation

Transformation is beautiful, but only in hindsight. At the moment, it feels like death, and in a way, it is. It's the death of what no longer serves you.

- Illusions' death.
- The death of the person you believed you needed to be.
- The death of "what ifs" and "what was."

But here's the sacred truth:

Everything God prunes, He intends to replace with fruit. Everything you release in obedience, He will multiply in grace.

Letting go isn't abandonment; it's acceptance. It's you saying, "God, I trust Your plan more than I trust my comfort. It won't always feel good, but it will always bear good fruit."

Letting go isn't just about people. It's about you.

Let go not only of a relationship but also of a version of yourself, moulded by survival instead of purpose.

- Embrace your true self, who speaks up.
- Nurture the person within who believes in herself.
- Celebrate the true you who shines without apology.
- Honour the true self that recognises its worth beyond merely being needed.

God treasures that version as well. Allow Him to remove your masks and draw you out of the shadows. Permit Him to burn away everything that isn't meant for where you're headed. This is the sacred pain of becoming.

Allow the tears to come freely.

Let the tears fall. If you're in a season where everything feels like it's slipping away, don't fight it. Don't hold it in. Let the tears flow freely. Grieve for the people who once walked closely with you but have now faded into the background. Grieve the version of yourself you no longer recognise, the one that existed before the growth, before the stretching, before the shift. Mourn the dreams that never materialised the way you hoped they would. Acknowledge the ache of the comfort you once depended on, the places and roles that once felt secure but no longer fit.

Then, rise, stand amid the ruins and look around. Understand this: God never permits the fire unless He plans to bring glory from the ashes. You are not being stripped to humiliate or punish you. You are being emptied so He can fill you with something greater, something eternal. This is not the end of your story; it's the sacred process of shedding one season so you can spread your wings in the next. Let go completely and finally, and allow what's no longer meant for you to fall away. Trust that what God removes, He intends to redeem. What expires in His hands will always give birth to something new.

Consider asking yourself:

- What am I still holding on to that no longer fits my future?
- Who or what am I afraid to let go—despite knowing it's time?
- Which version of myself must I surrender so God can raise the true me?

"Those who sow in tears will reap in joy."
Psalm 126:5

Let this chapter be the moment to let go of what was, so you can receive what is ahead, because God's plan for you is always greater than what you fear losing.

Reflective Journal

1. What painful experience changed how you see yourself or God? (Describe what happened and how it influenced your thinking.)
2. When have you grown the most, in comfort or pain? Why?

3. What thoughts or beliefs have you needed to unlearn to develop mental resilience?
4. How has your pain equipped you to support others? What message lies within your scars?
5. If your pain served a purpose, what do you think God intends to bring forth from it?

Letting go isn't abandonment; it's acceptance. It's you saying, "God, I trust Your plan more than I trust my comfort.

PART THREE

Overcoming Pain to Fulfil Destiny

Chapter 7

DEVELOPING A PAIN-RESILIENT MINDSET

Becoming Strong Enough to Carry Your Calling

"Weeping may endure for a night, but joy comes in the morning."

Psalm 30:5

Let's Start Here—What Is a Pain-Resilient Mindset?

A pain-resilient mindset is a way of thinking that allows you to persist despite experiencing pain. It's not about ignoring the pain, pretending to be happy, or quoting scriptures to conceal your feelings. Nor is it about being superhuman or emotionless.

It simply means this:

You have trained your mind to manage pain in a way that doesn't break you but helps you grow.

Consider it this way: in earthquake-prone areas, engineers include 'flexible foundations' in building designs. This enables the buildings to sway during ground shaking without breaking.

A pain-resistant mindset is your internal flexible foundation that sustains your faith, even when life destabilises everything else.

Shifting Your Perspective on Pain

Here is the truth you need to know:

Your perception of pain influences how you manage it.

Most of us grow up believing pain is something to avoid and that when life gets tough, it means something's wrong. But that belief is risky because when we face painful seasons (and we all will), we think:

- *Perhaps I overlooked God.*
- *Perhaps I am not capable.*
- *Perhaps quitting is the right move for me.*

But what if pain doesn't mean you're off-course? What if it is a regular part of growth?

Consider exercising. When you first go to the gym and start lifting weights, your muscles may feel sore. While this soreness can be uncomfortable, it also shows that you are building strength.

Pain in life often functions similarly. It's not there to kill you, but to stretch you, to build you, and to prepare you for what's ahead. However, this change won't happen automatically. You must train your mind to stop viewing pain as punishment and start perceiving it as preparation.

A Story to Help You Understand

Let's discuss Joseph from the Bible once more.

As a teenager, Joseph dreamt of becoming a prominent leader. But instead of ascending to power swiftly, his brothers betrayed him, threw him into a pit, sold him into slavery, falsely accused him, and imprisoned him.

At any point, Joseph could have said, "This dream was fake. My life is over." But he didn't. Why? Because somewhere along the way, Joseph developed a mindset that saw pain not as the end of the story but as part of the **process**.

When Joseph finally rose to power, he told his brothers, who had wronged him:

> *"You meant it for evil, but God meant it for good."*
> (Genesis 50:20)

That's a pain-resistant mindset.

Joseph realised something many of us overlook: pain is a tool God uses to guide you towards your purpose.

The Power of Endurance and Persistence

Let's simplify this approach:

- **Endurance is about persisting, even when it becomes difficult.**
- **Persistence means you keep going, even when you haven't seen results yet.**

Many people give up, not because they lack a calling, but because they didn't learn how to persevere through pain.

You recognise that even the most beautiful dreams encounter dark moments, and the most anointed individuals sometimes feel like giving up. Even Jesus, in the Garden of Gethsemane, said, "Father, if you are willing, take this cup from me." However, he didn't give up; he endured and persisted, and because of that, he brought **salvation to the world.** Sometimes, your most significant influence only materialises after enduring your toughest trials.

Practical Example: Enduring in Real Life

Suppose you start a business, but after a few months, you have no clients.

Or perhaps you're trying to rebuild your life after heartbreak, but you still wake up feeling empty. Or you're waiting for healing, yet it's been years, and nothing has changed. This is the crucial moment, the point at which pain might tempt you to give in, but if you have a pain-resilient mindset, you'll say:

- "I may not see the result yet, but I'm growing."
- "It still hurts, but I'm not stopping."
- "God is still writing my story, even though the silence."

That mindset distinguishes **those who live with regret from those who live in triumph.**

Transforming Pain into Meaningful Purpose

Let's be very clear about this: your pain was not random. There is something sacred about pain—something hidden within the heartbreak, loneliness, delays, and disappointments that life brings. Most of us go through painful seasons asking one question: "Why?"

- Why did they leave?
- Why did I lose that job?
- Why didn't the healing happen sooner?
- Why did God permit this?

But the "why" rarely uncovers purpose. The "what now?" uncovers purpose.

- What can I do with all I've experienced?
- Who can I assist with the lessons I've learned?
- How can I transform this wound into a source of wisdom?

The shift in perspective from asking "Why me?" to "How can this help someone else?" marks the start of transforming pain into purpose. Every betrayal, delay, loss, and every silent night; it wasn't just something you "went through"; it's something God will use to assist others through.

Purpose is Born in the Fire

Some of the most influential voices, leaders, and mentors worldwide are not those who lived perfect lives. Instead, they are the ones who endured the worst and refused to waste it.

- The woman, who was abused as a child, now runs a foundation supporting girls who have experienced abuse.
- Now advising teenagers on the brink is the man who once attempted to end his life.
- Now, supporting others to discover their identity in God is the girl who faced rejection.
- The widow, who once believed she wouldn't survive her grief, now writes books on healing for others.
- Becoming a voice for grieving mothers is the woman who lost her child.

- A man who overcame addiction starts a programme that saves thousands.
- Becoming a counsellor who helps teens heal is the girl who was bullied.

They didn't gain that purpose from a textbook; they found it through **the trenches of pain**. From nights of weeping, mornings of numbness, and long seasons where they believed nothing good could emerge from the chaos.

But here's the secret:

God does His best work with broken pieces.

God doesn't waste pain; we do!

You may not have control over what happened to you, but you have a choice in how to react. You can hide it, ignore it, or act like it didn't occur. However, eventually, you'll come to a realisation:

Unprocessed pain turns into poison, but pain that is released becomes strength.

When you surrender your story to God, a transformation occurs. He repurposes what broke you into something **that benefits others**. The tears you've shed in private now serve as fuel for your ministry. The parts of your life you'd prefer to forget become the bridges others will cross to discover their healing.

You ask, 'But it still hurts—so how does that help me?'

Let's be honest: transforming pain into purpose doesn't mean the pain vanishes. It means the pain serves you, rather than opposes you.

Here's how:

- It gives your suffering **meaning**. You understand, "This had a purpose."
- It provides your journey with **direction**. You now have clarity about what you're called to do.

- It leaves a mark on your life. Your story speaks, even when your mouth is silent.

Imagine a woman who has lost a child. No explanation can ease that kind of pain. But over time, God can grant her the strength to share her story and comfort other women who believe they are alone in their grief. In doing so**, the pain becomes a tool, not just a tragedy.**

Your Story Carries Healing

You don't have to be a preacher, author, or influencer to turn pain into purpose. If you've gone through something tough like divorce, illness, betrayal, addiction, or abandonment, and you're still here? You're a survivor.

That survival, when surrendered to God, becomes a **calling**.

- That thing you thought disqualified you? It might be what qualifies you to connect with others.

- The place where you experienced being crushed? It might be the soil in which your ministry develops.
- That moment you thought would destroy you? It could be the gateway to your greatest breakthrough.

God intends to redeem your pain, not only for your benefit but also for others who are waiting on the other side of your story.

People betrayed, beat, abandoned, mocked, and crucified Jesus, all for a purpose greater than the pain. And in His most profound suffering, a purpose was born for the entire world.

If Jesus endured pain to fulfil His mission, what makes us think we would not face similar struggles? Will purpose be born in comfort?

But here's the beauty:

If you walk with God through the pain, you won't just emerge; you will come out carrying power.

- Don't delay until you feel "qualified."
- Don't delay until you have everything figured out.

Start where you are, share your story and help someone who is hurting. Open your hands and say: "God, it still hurts, but if you can use it, take it."

That's where purpose starts.

You've cried, questioned, and nearly given up, but you're still here, and that alone shows me: you are a vessel of purpose.

The pain that tried to destroy you is the very thing God will use to **reveal you**. Let Him breathe on your brokenness. Allow Him to turn your ashes into beauty. Let Him turn your test into a testimony.

Your story is not finished, and it's about to reach the part that could transform someone else's life.

Building a Pain-Resilient Mindset

If you're wondering, "How can I apply this in real life?" remember that developing a pain-resilient mindset takes time. It's not something you achieve with a single prayer or overnight. Instead, it's a journey involving rewiring your thinking, responses, and approach to hardship. The goal is to strengthen your emotional, mental, and spiritual resilience so you can withstand pressure without breaking down whenever life becomes tough.

And let's be honest: life will get tough. But pain doesn't have to define you. You can train your mind to view pain differently. You can become someone who doesn't just survive storms, but grows through them.

Here's how you do it.

Step 1: Be Honest About the Pain

This marks the start of true healing. Stop pretending and downplay what you've been through. Stop saying,

"I'm fine," when you're falling apart inside.

God doesn't heal fake wounds; He heals genuine ones. Sometimes the bravest thing you can do is say:

- That shattered me.
- "I'm not okay."
- I feel forgotten, disappointed, angry, and exhausted.

You must recognise and name your pain to heal. Being honest isn't a sign of weakness; it's a sign of readiness.

Jesus our Lord in the Garden of Gethsemane groaned under the weight of what was to come. He didn't feign strength. He wept, He fell, and He asked the Father if there was another way.

But he also surrendered.

You must let your soul bleed before someone can bandage it. This is not emotional drama; it is spiritual surgery.

Step 2: Ask More Effective Questions

When pain strikes, people often ask themselves, "Why me?" However, this question rarely provides clarity. Instead, it fosters feelings of bitterness, blame, or shame.

A pain-resilient mindset asks a different question:

- God, what do You want to reveal to me through this?
- What now?
- What can develop from this place?

It's a slight change in perspective, but it opens the door to healing.

Imagine a gardener. When a tree isn't thriving, they don't shout at the leaves. They ask, "What's happening underground?" The same applies to you. Instead of dwelling on "why me," **ask questions that allow God to reveal, reshape, and redeem what's beneath the surface.**

Step 3: Speak Life Over Yourself

Pain has a voice, but so does your spirit. The one you feed the most will lead you. When you're in the middle of a storm, the enemy will whisper:

> 'You're finished; nothing will change; God has forgotten you.'

But a pain-resilient person learns to stand up for themselves. You don't deny the facts, but you declare the truth.

The **fact** is that you're tired, you're broke, and you're grieving.

God is your strength, your provider, and your comforter.

So you say:
- This hurts, but I am growing.
- I don't understand this, but I trust God anyway.
- This season won't defeat me; it's shaping me.
- Something positive will result from this.

The power of life and death is in your tongue. (Proverbs 18:21). Train your mouth **to speak hope**, not merely pain.

Step 4: Stay Connected to God

The enemy's aim during painful seasons is not only to hurt you but also to separate you from God, make you feel alone, and persuade you that God has forsaken you.

But it's through the pain that you must press in, not pull away.

- Stay in the Word, even if it feels dry.
- Keep praying, even if tears come.
- Continue worshipping even when you lack motivation.

Because here's the secret: God is most present in your pain. He may seem silent, but He is not absent. And He does His deepest work in the darkest places.

Think of Job. In his suffering, he said:

> "Though He slay me, yet will I trust Him."
>
> (Job 13:15)

That's not denial. That's **deep faith.** If you stay close to God in the storm, you won't just survive it; you will emerge with **wisdom, authority, and intimacy** you never had before.

Step 5: Keep Moving

Sometimes, pain makes you want to freeze, maybe to shut down and give up. But a pain-resilient person says:

> "I may crawl, but I'm still moving."

You don't need to run; you don't have to have everything sorted**, but don't stop.**

In the case you're writing a book, write a paragraph each day. If you're starting over, take one step towards healing. If you're rebuilding your life, wake up, make your bed, and choose to show up.

Momentum is a spiritual weapon. The more you move forward, the less power pain has over you.

David says, "Even though I walk through the valley of the shadow of death..." (Psalm 23:4). He didn't pitch a tent in the valley. He **walked through** it.

So must you.

- You're not weak for facing difficulties.
- You're not faithless for experiencing pain.
- The statement that you are human is true. And you are healing.

Building a pain-resilient mindset is not about pretending you're unshakable; it's about becoming **rooted** in truth, even when the winds blow. So when life hits hard again, and it will, you'll say:

- Despite the tough situations I've faced, I'm still standing.
- Trust doesn't require understanding.
- I'm not breaking; I am being built.

Because God has not finished with you, He is developing you. And this season is not at the end; this is your season of becoming equipped.

You are stronger than you know.

Pain can deceive you, making you believe you're weak, broken, and that you'll never recover. But here's the truth:

As long as you're breathing, you're still growing. If you're still standing, it means God hasn't finished with you yet.

You may feel you're walking through fire right now, but remember, fire refines gold. Even if you think your story ended, pressure creates diamonds. You may feel lost, but perhaps this isn't the end—perhaps it's becoming your true self.

There is no need for you to be perfect; allow God to use your pain to shape you. **Trust the process to foster growth**, and let tears flow if needed. After crying, stand up again, because those destined for greatness are not the ones who never experience pain—they are the ones who choose to grow through it.

Chapter 8

HEALING WHILE WALKING

Finding Strength in Faith and Spirituality

"As they went, they were healed."

Luke 17:14

When Life Doesn't Pause for Your Pain

Sometimes life hits you so hard you wish you could vanish, but you can't. You still have mouths to feed, emails to answer, bills to pay, people to care for, and deadlines to meet. You're still required to face life, regardless of whether your heart feels prepared.

This makes the pain feel even heavier. It's not just the wound; it's the pressure to keep living as if you're not bleeding inside.

- No sabbatical.
- No time-out.
- No dramatic "fade to black" so the healing can happen offstage.

It's real life. For many of us, real life involves learning to heal as we go. But here's the sacred truth most cannot recognise:

Healing isn't always a quiet process; sometimes, it happens through movement.

The lepers received healing while walking.

Recall the 10 lepers in Luke 17 who met Jesus. They were unclean, rejected, and unwanted. They ask Jesus for healing, and instead of performing a ritual or speaking elaborate words, Jesus simply says, "*Go. Show yourselves to the priests.*"

They were still not healed. They remained ill, broken, and disqualified by religious law. Yet Jesus told them to move forward as if they were already clean.

That's faith, and here's the miracle:

> "As they went, God healed them."

Not before, not after. '**As they walked.**'

Healing occurred through their movement. It came by choosing obedience, not when the pain ceased, but when they opted to move, regardless.

> 'You Don't Have to Be Whole to Move Forward,'

We've been taught that healing comes before action. That we need to "get ourselves together" before we obey, serve, lead, or love again. But God does not operate on that timeline. Some of the most transformative seasons of your life will happen **while you're still in pain.**

- You'll be building while bleeding.
- Leading while limping.
- Trusting while trembling.
- Showing up to work with a shattered heart.
- Ministering with tears in your eyes.
- Raising kids while grieving your lost childhood.
- Starting over, even though part of you still misses what broke you.

This is not a flaw. This is how becoming happens.

How Faith Sustains You in Painful Seasons

Faith is not simply a feeling. It's not the absence of fear. Faith is **the choice to continue walking with God**, even when you do not know where the path leads.

Faith doesn't remove pain; it provides a stable place to stand when everything else is shaking. It isn't a magical escape from hardship but a sacred anchor that prevents your soul from drifting into despair.

Pain can resemble a storm. Sometimes it strikes suddenly, like a doctor's diagnosis, a betrayal, losing a job, or a broken home. At other times, it gradually seeps in, enveloping your mind and causing you to question your worth, direction, and purpose.

And in those moments, logic isn't sufficient. You can't think your way out of heartbreak; you can't even research your way through grief, nor can you analyse your way past trauma.

All you require is faith.

It's trusting that:

- Even during His silence, God remains with you.
- Your suffering is acknowledged; that's the point.
- This pain serves a purpose.

There's a reason Scripture says, "The just shall live by faith." There are seasons when **faith is all you possess.** Perhaps:

- You do not know how the bills will be settled.
- You don't know how the relationship will be mended.
- You can't imagine joy coming back into your life.

But something deep inside urges, "*Keep walking. God's not done yet.*"

That is faith. It is what sustains you through sleepless nights, unexpected losses, and unanswered prayers. And that faith? It's far from being called small. This faith is challenging to break. **It's miraculous.**

Faith Is Trust in a God You Can't Always Feel

When you are suffering, God can seem distant, silent, and even far away. When you pray, the heavens feel closed. You read Scripture, and the words feel dry. You sing in church, but your heart remains numb.

But hear this:

> *Faith is choosing to believe God is near, even when your emotions can't detect Him.*

It's based on the truth of who He is, not the uncertainty of what you feel.

Faith says:

- Although I don't see how this will end, I know who holds the pen.
- Even though the future is uncertain, I know I'm not alone.
- Even though I don't feel peaceful, I believe peace is coming.

Faith Is a Quiet, Steady Yes

We often think of faith as loud shouting, jumping, and prophesying. But the faith that sustains you through pain is seldom dramatic.

It is quiet. It is the faith that softly whispers:

Just one more step, just one more breath, just one more prayer.

Faith in painful seasons is often invisible to others. You don't post about it. You don't always talk about it. But deep in your soul, you've made a choice:

I will not cease believing, even when I am bleeding.

That decision, that resolute, sacred yes, is what heaven endorses.

Faith Keeps You Grounded When Emotions Deceive

Pain lies to you. It tells you that you are alone or that you will never get through this. It can even tell you that God doesn't care for you, or that this is the end. But faith answers back:

He affirmed that He would never leave me nor forsake me. We can always find him near the broken-hearted. He has said to me that everything works together for my good, and I am more than a conqueror.

Faith reminds you that *'what you're walking through is temporary'*, but the promises of God are eternal.

When grief floods your soul, faith becomes your lifeboat. When shame whispers you're disqualified, faith says grace still qualifies you, and when life makes no sense, faith says, *"Even this has purpose."*

Faith doesn't prevent the fire—it carries you through it

The three Hebrew boys in Daniel 3 didn't escape the fire; however, because of their faith, they walked through it and emerged without even smelling of smoke.

They said to the king:

> *"Even if our God does not rescue us, we will not bow."*

That's faith. Not just believing in the miraculous, but believing, even if the miracle doesn't happen as you expect.

And guess what? God was in the fire with them. He hadn't met them *before*, and He didn't pull them *out* immediately. He joined them **in the flames**.

Faith enables you to recognise the Fourth Man in your furnace.

Faith doesn't rush God; it rests in God.

Pain makes us impatient, to the point where we seek answers now. We desire healing now. We crave closure now.

But faith says:

- Despite the delay, He is working.
- His presence remains, even in silence.
- His goodness remains, even in loss.

Faith trusts in **God's character** when His timeline doesn't seem to align. Just as Abraham waited decades for a promised child, Hannah returned year after year to the temple, and Jesus Himself endured Gethsemane, saying, "Not My will, but Yours be done."

Faith may not remove the wait, but it keeps your heart soft **while you wait.**

Faith Turns Survival into Strength

If you're still breathing, you've already endured more than you imagined you could. And guess what?

That was faith. You just didn't realise it.

You kept waking up, praying, forgiving, and believing, even when you were in doubt. That is faith in its rawest form.

And now, that faith is transforming pain into resilience.

- You're not merely surviving; you're building resilience.
- You are not merely enduring; you are developing.
- You're not merely holding on — you're being held.

Faith achieves that.

You might say: But my faith is weak, and some days I can hardly believe.

Listen: it's not the size of your faith that sustains you; it's the size of your God.

Jesus says, *"If you have faith the size of a mustard seed…"* That's all it takes. So even if all you can say today is:

God, help me. I don't understand, but I trust you, and I am still here.

That is enough. He sees every tear, He hears every whispered prayer, and honours every trembling step you take forward. Faith doesn't make life easy. But it gives the pain a purpose.

So don't let go of faith, even if it's trembling and questioned, because that thread of faith pulls you towards your healing.

The Role of Prayer, Meditation, and Divine Guidance

When you're going through emotional pain, your mind can feel chaotic, with endless thoughts of doubt, fear, regret, and despair. That's why spiritual practises are essential, not optional—they serve as vital lifelines.

Prayer is how you bleed in the presence of God without shame. It is where you tell Him the truth and not the filtered version, **but the raw one**.

Prayer is where you tell God, 'I am hurting... I don't understand... Please hold me today.'

Meditation helps train your heart to find peace amidst chaos. By repeatedly reflecting on scripture truths until they are ingrained, breathing through anxious moments, and anchoring yourself in eternal truths rather than fleeting feelings, you develop a stable foundation.

Divine guidance becomes essential in this sphere. Pain often urges you to make hasty decisions. But when you stay close to the Holy Spirit, He directs you wisely, even when your emotions cry out otherwise.

Let God guide you through the fog. He knows the turn ahead.

You're Not the Only One Who's Walked Bleeding

Many people you admire today—preachers, authors, mentors, leaders—were not always resilient. They learned to keep going despite being wounded.

- The pastor who teaches thousands survived depression in silence for years.
- While fighting unresolved trauma, the mother raised leaders.
- Inspiring crowds now, the speaker once curled up in bed, praying to disappear.
- Imposter syndrome whispered lies daily to the CEO as they built a brand.

They were not superhuman; they simply refused to give up but trusted God step by step, and you can do the same.

Healing isn't always what you expect it to be.

You may expect one big emotional breakthrough. One church service where everything lifts. One word from someone that makes it all better.

But often, healing is:

- Showing up daily, irrespective of hardship, displays a quiet strength.
- Crying while preparing a warm, comforting dinner, and allowing emotions to mix with the familiar scents of home, represents bittersweet moments.
- Grappling with doubt and uncertainty while reading Scripture is a challenge, especially when seeking comfort in words that once offered clarity.
- The raw honesty of saying "I forgive" through clenched teeth, battling the heaviness of resentment while yearning for release.

- *Like a gentle tide washing away fears and anxieties again and again, the decision to repeatedly choose peace remains.*

Healing isn't always loud. Sometimes it's **quiet victories** that no one sees, but Heaven sees and rewards the faithful ones who keep walking.

A Word of Grace: You Won't Bleed Forever

There will come a day when the tears that once flowed every day will fade into distant echoes, the memories that pierced your heart will soften, their sharpness dulled by time, the weight you've borne will gradually lighten, lifting like a heavy fog, and the radiant light will once again dance in your eyes, illuminating your spirit.

It may not happen today or next week, but one day, you'll look back and say:

> *That almost broke me. But it didn't. And look at me now.*

You will share your story to comfort others. You will create something beautiful from the ruins; you will breathe more deeply, love more fully, and live more freely.

For now, continue walking, even if you limp, feel hollow, or don't understand, because healing is happening as you move forward.

Final Encouragement

If you're walking through a painful season, let this be your reminder:

- Being completely healed is unnecessary for obeying God.
- Being useful doesn't require you to be powerful.
- Being whole isn't a requirement for progression.

God is not waiting for perfection; He's partnering with your surrender. So take another step today, whisper one more prayer, and open your heart just a little wider. Believe that this season, no matter how painful, is working for your good.

Because while you're walking…**God is healing.**

Reflective Journal

1. What pain are you currently carrying while still trying to function in life?
   (Be honest with yourself — where are you bleeding while still walking?)
2. In what ways have you seen healing happen as you moved forward, even before you felt ready?
3. What does walking by faith look like for you in this season of pain?
   (Describe a step of obedience you've taken, even while hurting.)
4. Where have you seen God's presence quietly sustain you during your lowest moments?
5. What is one truth about God that you are choosing to believe, even if your feelings haven't caught up yet?

Chapter 9

SURROUNDING YOURSELF WITH THE RIGHT PEOPLE

Because Destiny Isn't a Solo Journey

"Show me your friends, and I'll show you your future."

That quote may sound cliché, but it's startlingly accurate. The people surrounding you can either uplift you into your purpose or gradually suppress your destiny, and you may not notice until it's almost too late.

Pain teaches us many things, but one of its most profound lessons is this:

- You cannot heal in every environment.
- You cannot grow in every soil.
- You cannot thrive in every circle.

There are rooms where you feel alive, seen, pushed and covered. There are also rooms where something shrinks your spirit, where silence, sarcasm, or subtle jealousy meet your dreams.

This chapter is about learning to **discern** the difference. And more importantly, it's about finding the courage to **make the right choices.**

Why You Need Mentors and Destiny Helpers

You should not walk this journey alone. Jesus didn't. Disciples, friends, and encouragers supported him. He had John to lean on in Gethsemane. He had Mary to anoint Him before burial, and He had Simon to carry the cross when He could no longer stand.

You may be strong, gifted, and called. But even the most anointed individuals need support.

You need:

- Someone who has been where you're heading.
- Someone capable of hearing God even when your mind is clouded.
- Someone who can support you by holding your arms when you're too exhausted to keep praying.
- Someone who will support you, even when you're not performing.

These are **mentors** and **destiny helpers.** You receive no flattery from them. There is no competition between you and them. They don't fear your growth. They stand in the background, planting, pruning, pushing, and praying. And when you find one? Something in your soul exhaling will be the way you know. You will feel both *challenged* and *safe*. You will feel seen, not just for who you are, but for **who you are becoming.**

The Stranger Who Knew My Future

One day, I recall sitting at the back of a quiet seminar. I didn't know why I had come. I felt overlooked, confused about my direction, and honestly, a little lost.

Then, during a break, a woman I'd never met sat next to me. She looked at me, paused, and whispered:

> *There's something in your life. I don't know what you've been through, but you will not stay there. I'd like to walk with you for a while.*

During that moment, it felt like heaven had descended to whisper, "You are not forgotten."

She did not offer me a flashy opportunity; she simply **stayed.** She corrected me, listened carefully, and created space for me. Over time, God used her to lay the foundation on which I now stand.

That's what a destiny helper looks like. A title isn't necessary for them; they are not loud, but strategic. They are not always forever, but are there for the right season.

Recognising Toxic Influences That Hinder Growth

Just as important as finding the right people, it's equally vital to spot the wrong ones.

Toxic relationships are like spiritual smoke; you may not see the flames immediately, but the longer you breathe it in, the more difficult it becomes to function.

Sometimes it's a friend who:

- They laugh when you share your dream, but they never support it.
- Gaslights your pain and tells you to "just get over it."
- Lures you back into old habits each time you attempt to move forward.
- It stirs drama or negativity just when you're finally finding peace.

Sometimes, toxicity isn't confrontational; it's passive. It's the person who never celebrates you, the one who competes silently. They are the ones who secretly take pleasure in your struggles.

And here's what's most dangerous:

You can become so accustomed to dysfunctional people that healthy ones feel strange.

But when God is preparing you for a new season, He will start shifting your circle. Some people will fall away. Don't chase them. That is not punishment; that is protection.

Building a Circle That Strengthens You

Imagine your destiny as a delicate seed resting in your hand. If you plant it in dry, cracked earth, it won't grow, regardless of its strength. But in the right soil, with the proper water, sunlight, and cover? It blossoms.

The same is true for you; surround yourself with people who:

- Pray with you, not only for you.
- Speak life into your identity, not fear into your future.
- Tell you the truth, even when it hurts, but in love.
- Do not need to be seen beside you to be rooting for you.

Building this kind of circle takes time and effort. It calls for intention, prayer, and discernment. You may need a period of solitude to develop into someone who values quality over quantity. That's perfectly fine.

'It is better to walk alone with God than run with a crowd headed nowhere.'

An Emotional Word for the Wounded

If you've ever experienced betrayal by someone you trusted, I understand your feelings. Whether your best friend became a stranger, your prayer partner turned into your gossip target, or your "ride-or-die" left you when you needed them most, you're not alone. Jesus also went through similar situations.

- Judas betrayed Him.
- Peter denied Him.
- Most of the disciples *ran away* when He needed them most.

Yet, He continued to love and pursue His purpose. Don't allow a single heartbreak to harden your heart. Don't let one season of betrayal make you mistrust all the divine relationships God intends to bring.

Healing is achievable, and safe individuals exist.

Reflective Journal

Choose People Who Feed What's Growing in You

This season is sacred, and we must safeguard sacred things. Be honest with yourself and ask yourself these questions:

- Who brings peace when someone invades my space?
- Which person makes you feel exhausted?

- When nobody is watching, who prays with you?
- Who gives you faith, and who gives you fear?

You don't need perfect individuals, but present, purposeful, and prayerful ones. Let go of those who cannot celebrate your journey and treasure the few who recognise who you're becoming—sometimes even before you do. Remember, destiny is too burdensome to carry alone, and God never intended for you to do so.

...Destiny is too burdensome to carry alone, and God never intended for you to do so.

Chapter 10

THIS IS WHAT BECOMING LOOKS LIKE

*You've overcome it for a reason —
now stand tall and rise.*

There comes a moment in every journey through pain when something shifts, not around you, but within you. It doesn't always happen with fireworks or fanfare. Sometimes it's just a deep breath in the silence. A quiet moment where you realise:

I'm still here.

After all the breaking, the isolation, the betrayal, the waiting, the letting go: yes, you're still standing, still breathing, and still believing. And for the first time in a long while, perhaps even ever, you don't just see the pain; you know what it has created.

It didn't destroy you; it revealed who you are. This is what it means to become.

Becoming doesn't begin on a stage. It doesn't start when you launch the ministry, write the book, get the promotion, or marry the love of your life. Becoming begins in the dark, in the dirt, and in the silent, unseen seasons where no one sees the tears, but God is shaping you.

Like a seed buried underground, the work happens before anyone cheers. Roots before fruit. Depth before visibility.

There were moments you believed someone buried you, but in truth, someone planted you.

And now... the breaking was not the end. It was a beginning.

You didn't just make it — it made you.

Consider a diamond. Before it shines, it endures intense, crushing, and prolonged pressure. Not because it's worthless, but because this pressure is necessary to reveal its brilliance.

"You are the diamond."

Reflect on gold. It must endure fire to distinguish the pure from the impure. The fire isn't a punishment; it's a refiner.

You are gold!

The things that broke others moulded you into your present self. What destroyed others deepened you. What delayed others developed you.

You didn't just survive pain.

"Pain revealed the greatness inside you."

You are not the same person you were back then. Take a moment to look at yourself.

- You are wiser.
- Not weaker, but gentler, is what you are.
- Rather than tougher, you are more substantial.
- Your love is more profound.
- Your vision is clearer.
- Trust comes slower to you, but forgiveness comes quicker.
- Things you once tolerated are no longer acceptable.
- There's no need to justify yourself to those not in your destiny.
- You don't pursue what doesn't choose you.
- You don't settle for less. You now have an awareness of your identity.

That's not arrogance. That's what healing feels like.

It All makes Sense

There comes a point when you cease questioning, "Why did this happen to me?" and instead ask, "How can God use this in me?" This is the moment you stop defining your life by the chapter that hurt you, and instead start writing a chapter that brings redemption. The purpose of pain is not to hold you back; it is to elevate you into clarity, calling, and conviction.

Now, you say:

- That heartbreak was a gateway.
- That rejection was redirection.
- That silence served as training.
- "That loneliness was preparation."
- That delay was divine.

This is the moment where you say:

> *I understand now. God was not neglecting me. He was shaping me.*

You Are Becoming

Becoming is not a destination; it is a process, and you are in it right now.

You're becoming:

- A woman aware of her value.
- A man who walks in wisdom.
- A compassionate leader.
- A mother breaking cycles passed down through generations.
- A mentor who offers support from the surplus of healing.
- A voice of authority that bears truth because it has experienced pain.

This isn't just about what happened to you; this is about who you *became* because of it.

Scars That Narrate a Story

You may carry scars, not all of them visible. Some are emotional, and others spiritual, but they don't disqualify you; they **validate** you. Your scars are a testament to the fact that you've been through something and *survived*. And more than survived... You *overcame*.

Wear them with humility, not as symbols of shame, but of strength.

Because when you speak from your scars, others find **hope** in their wounds.

You survived, so you could:

- Speak.
- Serve.
- Lead.
- Write.
- Build.
- Teach.
- Heal.

You must not return to your old self. You are called to **emerge**, to **elevate**, and to **walk confidently in your calling**. This is not your comeback; this is your becoming, and no one can take it away from you.

Final Word of Encouragement

From My Heart to Yours

If you've reached this point, take a moment to pause and breathe. Not just a shallow breath, but a deep, genuine, healing one.

Allow it to fill your lungs, clear your mind, and remind your soul:

- *You made it.*
- Through the fire.
- Through the silence.
- Through the tears that no one saw.
- Through the goodbyes, you never explained.
- Through the nights, you thought you wouldn't survive.

You didn't just read a book. You went on a journey, and, more importantly, you journeyed through it by yourself. I understand what it's like to feel broken beyond recognition, to stand in front of the mirror and not recognise yourself anymore. What about when you lose things? I understand what it feels like to experience loss. People, parts of yourself, and to wonder if you will ever recover. I know how to love God deeply, yet I still question whether He sees you.

But I also know this:

- There is glory to come after this.
- Joy returns once more.
- There is a rising strength within your soul, even now.
- There is a purpose so profound in your life that the pain had to come first, just to make space for it.

You are not beyond repair; you are being **reconstructed with purpose**. God didn't waste a single tear; He didn't miss a single cry. He was working behind the scenes, even when you thought He had walked away.

The fire didn't burn you down; it burned away what couldn't go with you.

So rise, not hurried, not perfect. Not entirely figured out. Just willing. Willing to believe that everything you've walked through was not merely a valley, but a birthing ground.

You are becoming something beautiful.

Someone powerful.

Someone purposeful.

And someone who will now help others walk out of their pain, too.

You're not alone; you never were. And from this day forward, you never have to pretend again. Your scars are not your shame; they are your story, and someone needs your voice. Someone needs your healing. Someone needs your light.

So don't dim it. Don't run from the pain that gave it life. Don't doubt the God who permitted it, solely because He intends to use it.

This is what it feels like to fulfil your destiny. It can be painful, but it's worth the struggle.

And so are you.

With love,
Omolabake Olaoye

www.ingramcontent.com/pod-product-compliance
Lightning Source LLC
Chambersburg PA
CBHW050805160426
43192CB00010B/1648